All Shapes and Sizes

Poems
by
Lynn Skapyak Harlin

Copyright ©2022 by Lynn Skapyak Harlin

All rights reserved by the author. No part of this publication may be reproduced, stored in a retrieval system, or transmitted in any form or by any means (electronic, photocopy, mechanical, recording or otherwise) without prior permission of the author with the exception of brief quotations in critical reviews and articles.

Cover painting by Rhiannon Lee
Layout by Richard Levine
"Dead Weight" appeared in *Age Changes*, 2017

First Edition, September, 2022

Published by Hidden Owl, LLC,
hiddenowl.com

ISBN 978-0-9962371-9-2

Printed in the United States of America

For my daughter, Rhiannon Lee,
who lights up my life.

Contents

Acknowledgments...ix
Introduction..xi
Getting It Out..1
Sifting My Past..2
Stagnant...4
She Brings Changes..5
Guardians...6
An Editor in Saba..7
Passing...8
Bright Young Men...9
Dragonfly on Blanding Blvd..10
Watching the Contrast..11
It Isn't Easy...14
Colors My Day..15
Gwendolyn Brooks..16
Suburban Suite...18
Wildlife Officer Kills Snakes at I-75 Rest Area.................19

Poetry Forms..21
The Rondelet..22
All Shapes and Size..23
Richie Levine..23
The Cinquain..24
Feline..25
Writer..25
Woman..25
Maureen..25
The Tanka...26
white lightning..27
3 tankas for Jim..27
Pain smacks...27

Dreary day	27
Winter sunny day	27
The Triolet	28
Some Days Some Nights	29
Smiles	29
My Dentures	29
The Haiku	30
brown dust	31
eye holder	31
hands behind	31
loud screech	31
gray moss	31
high brown	31
The Clerihew	32
Paula R. Hilton	33
Jim Draper	33
Anne Perry	33
Alan Bradley	33
The Pantoum	34
Poets Pantoum	35
Flamingos, Dragons and Dragonflies	36
PC ah PC with a Maule	38
May 1996	40
Seeking Solace	41
His Leaving	42
Death Drive to Dallas and Back	44
Lovely Ladies	**45**
Elizabeth	47
Allison	48
Beth	50
Lisa	52

Martha 54
Trying 56
at 75 All the Same 57
No More Good Moves 58
Hubird and Liz 59
Summer Daze 60
Murder Mouse 61
Skeleton Remnants 62
Stars on Water 63
My Gratitude List 64
Flickers Dance 65
A Gentle Nag 66
Dead Weight 67
Rusty Spigot 68
Cauldron of Thoughts 69
Eggs Boiling and Aging 70
at 76 Hopeful 71
Name Changes 72
Just Now 73
George 74
Never Did Understand 75
Old Friends Gone 76
at 77 Seeking Joy 77

About the Author 78
Books Edited by Lynn Skapyak Harlin 80

Acknowledgments

Love and thanks to my husband, Jim Harlin, for encouraging me to put my poems together in this collection.

Special thanks to fellow poet, Paula R. Hilton for reading the poems in *All Shapes and Sizes* and giving me excellent feedback. Her help made this book better.

Gratitude and appreciation for my friend and colleague Richie Levine who always makes my writing look good.

Introduction

Most storage units are filled with unremarkable things. Outdated textbooks from college, abandoned treadmills, and boxes upon boxes of clothes. But a rare few contain hidden treasures. The book you hold in your hands now is one of them.

In May of 2022, renowned North Florida poet, Lynn Skapyak Harlin, faced the monumental task of emptying a unit she'd maintained for decades. Amongst the expected items she ended up donating or discarding, she discovered poems. Vibrant pieces of her past, as alive in the drafts she found as the day she wrote them, greeted her inside bin after bin. In "Sifting My Past," she states:

My thoughts rush and tumble.
Read a letter, find a photo
see a face, suddenly with
them, in that time and place.

In Lynn's second full length poetry collection, *All Shapes and Sizes*, she invites us to time travel with her. To meet the fascinating people she's known and loved, some still in her life, some not. All cherished. In a section of her book titled "Lovely Ladies" we get to know Elizabeth:

She leads with high laugh,
deep red lipstick,
tattooed skin, arrayed in
flowing black clothes.
Alert mind, open intently
listening, befriending
crones, older women
with much to share.

And share Lynn does. Like Elizabeth, I have the great fortune to be one of the many beneficiaries of her expertise and generosity. I first met Lynn in 2017, when I was a student in her Shantyboat Writers Workshop. After only a few months of lessons with Lynn, short stories and poems I'd been sending out for years were accepted for publication. Lynn showed me that what you leave out of a piece is as important as what you share. She taught me not to waste words. Too many and they lose their power. In "at 75 All the Same" she writes:

Her brain sizzles pops and
cracks as she turns each
lettered page waiting for her
pencil to scratch out words,
move sentences around
look for the inner core.
Can the story be found?

In 2019, my husband asked me what I wanted for my birthday. My answer? An editor. And not just any editor. I knew if she agreed to take me on Lynn Skapyak Harlin would help me to create a book of poems I'd be proud to see in print. She did this and so much more. When poets work with Lynn, they not only get the sharpest-eyed of editors, they also gain a professional writing teacher. Lynn immediately noticed I wrote only in free verse. She began emailing me lessons on how to create poems of all shapes and sizes. Within a month, she had me writing my first Villanelle, a Pantoum, a Cinquain, a Triolet and several Tankas. Of course, you'll find all these classical forms and more, in this collection. While I love and admire each of them, I have a favorite, "Poets Pantoum."

Poets see what others miss
they write their thoughts to share
wet leaf glistens with sun's kiss,
oh, look closely if you dare.

In Thornton Wilder's *Our Town*, Emily asks the stage manager, "Do any human beings ever realize life while they live it—every minute?" He replies, "No—saints and poets, maybe—they do some." While Lynn Skapyak Harlin would gleefully tell you in her legendary smoky voice that she's no saint, there's also no doubt she's one of the rare writers who dares to pay attention. Lynn looks at life, the past and present, at every moment, in all its pain. In all its beauty.

Her masterful collection, *All Shapes and Sizes*, urges all of us to do the same.

Paula R. Hilton,
author of *At Any Given Second* and *Little Miss Chaos*
August 2, 2022

Getting It Out

She always finds it best to
get things out in the open
early in a conversation.
Beating around the bush is
only useful when hunting.

It slows down the progress,
stops the contact, diverts
purpose, causes impatience.
Instead she is direct in her
dealings with people.

Some call her outspoken,
others think she is obnoxious,
yet to the dear blessed few
she is honest, sincere—
an authentic woman.

Sifting My Past

We emptied a storage unit,
file cabinets filled with old
treasures, 20 boxes, 5 rubber
bins, 40 black garbage
bags, to discard or keep.
Each file must be opened
each page examined,
find personal info, checks,
bills, pay stubs to shred.
Parts of poems started,
drafts left for decades,
now need to be finished.

I am tired, drained but curious.
My thoughts rush and tumble.
Read a letter, find a photo
see a face, suddenly with
them, in that time and place.

I am lucky, time to sift files,
find validation, proof of the
things I have done: flew a plane,
drove tractor trailer, from NYC,
to Mexico City, Phoenix, Montreal,
sailed on a tjalk (chalik) in Dutch seas,
to the Dutch and German Islands,
crossed the Atlantic on the
William R. Adams, so many
class lesson plans I wrote, taught.

Time to think of places
I've been: drove and flew
across this country, from
Boston to San Francisco,
went around the world
with Ross Perot, lived in
the Netherlands, stayed
in Saba, slept in Morocco
took buses and trains
through Europe, on my own.

Time to read so many cards,
so many letters from people,
I loved, some still in my
life, still alive, some dead.
Time to renew friendships.

Time to sift through my
past is essential now
I am getting older,
slowing down, not doing
much, not going nor taking
those adventures, I took before.

Stagnant
San Francisco, May 1972

My writing is getting
stagnant, like me,
still and boring.
I'm not growing.
I sit and watch, wait
for sunshine, to warm,
to wake me, right me.
Midday slow driving
over the Golden Gate.
Looking down, seeing
sailboats, sails furling
sharp sloop chopping
through waves roiling
dark blue green,
Pacific water moving
words out of me.

She Brings Changes
Fernandina, 1979

Nothing ever stays the same.
It is only letting the changes,
change you. It is just sitting
back and letting whoever take
control. You aren't you now,
you aren't still in command.

She is spitting at the smell
my sweating body makes.
I type on and thank God for
Mr. Rogers, he pulls her
spit away. Out of her chair
she calls, "Mom," now at
my side she climbs my back,
pinching cheeks and pulling
my jersey. "Mine," she says
as she grasps my left nipple,
"Mine." She is in charge now,
my charge, her needs rule me.
Changes, she is changes for me.

Some moments are not swell,
oh, damn some changes are hell.

Guardians

There are those white skinned,
white haired ladies, who stand
straight, red tight lips pursed,
who guard parking spaces in
crowded asphalt shopping plazas.
They are the shouters,
"Millie," she starts at a mild
shriek, "Millieee," she screams
impatiently, until she's found.
They are grandmothers, who buy
by the sales. They stand perfumed
in ready to wear knit pantsuits.
They are mothers of disheveled,
harried, jean clad women, like me.
At photo specials, they dare me to
usurp their turf. To push my cart
too close, to touch their pile of
precious purchases picked by
them. Guardians they are,
warding, shooing, me off.

An Editor in Saba
Netherland, Antilles

Ned, in 1982
it is like you:
hidden treasure
isolated volcanic
getaway, few
tourists touch down
land, stay here
trek craggy slopes
see rare tropical blooms
savor exotic aromas
sensual breeze
flavored dining
delicacies served
overlooking the Caribbean.
Captain's Quarters
clings to lush hillside
a prize soothing
an end finished
on small Saba.

Passing

Sometimes when we pass a tight
bottomed eighteen-year-old and
I'm worried whether or not you
are thinking about her, that's when
a car will pass and two eyes are
level with mine and a mouth will
spread at the corners, smile wide.
I smile back and start wondering.

Bright Young Men

Be aware,
of bright young men.
Be wary,
of them who speak
with older women.
Beware
of the young man who
chooses an older woman.
Be wary,
older women of
bright young men.
Be aware,
of the one bright
young man, who makes
a bright older woman
weary.

Dragonfly on Blanding Blvd.

A dragonfly flickered
    through Friday traffic on
Blanding Boulevard.
This road stacks cars up making
  a labyrinth for this flittering.
It was just barely above the
    autos, not even over the
antennae.
      Moving zig zag slow.
I waited as the light changed,
    only saw metal stirring.
Did you make it to the woods?
     Flashing, flickering,
flittering on
    Blanding Boulevard,
wings gleaming,
    glistening, glittering
  flickering, flittering
    rush hour dragonfly.

Watching the Contrast

Living in Lakewood, June 1982
watching the contrast of two ages.
She dances gaily from rooms. While
her 82-year-old gait is a marked shuffle
heard at night, moving steadfastly
toward the bathroom, plodding
resolutely back to her blue room.
There are moments when her world is clear.

Sometimes her shuffle to the toilet is
punctuated by a burst of backfires
telling her to hurry. Fleeing in terror
her shaky voice asks, "Where is the
toilet?" Each time she inquires,
most times she is quick enough.

"How come Nana Trudeau is the head
of the family, she can't even find the
bathroom, Ma?" great granddaughter asks.
I have no answers, I'm somewhere in the
middle of the shuffle and the dance.
I see it all, hear the laughter, feel the
pain and wonder, "What comes next?"

We are three women, four generations apart.
I am overwhelmed, but once you realize
you can't and won't do anything to change
it, you just go on bitching and whining
and complaining and just go on.

Nana changes clothes some nights like
she's readying for a first date.
Does she have a destination as she
labors over fastening her corset at 4:00 a.m.?
I've asked and she merely shakes her head,
says, "How silly of me. I feel so foolish."
Poor, proud lady she often feels foolish.
We only giggle slyly here and tell her
how helpful she is, as she pulls the elastic
band from her five-year-old offshoot's hair.
"Nana doesn't hurt like you do, Mom."
Rhiannon says the right thing, sometimes.

Daily bouts with pains unclear to her and us.
The older one has an ache in her back,
sharp pain here, a belch from her mouth,
a sudden, loud fart from her rear,
stray sounds made for all to hear.

Her life is reduced to eating
"as a savage," her words often
said after a favorite meal or "a
genteel sufficiency" which usually
follows the meal she just wolfs down.
My grandmother eats, revels in eating.
She will declare she is starving if you
forget to feed her every three hours.

Nana walks often, feverishly at times.
She is haunted by the "there must be
something I must be doing," demon.
He plagues mothers widowed with
six kids under seven. He plagues
others too, but this type I know.
Nana scouts the living room carpet
pile for stray bits of lint for her
eyes to light on to stoop and
creakingly relieve rug of its
extra tufts. She is skilled
at this strenuous task.

In the "home" where she
resided for three weeks,
they tired of watching her
treks and tied her to chairs.
Encased her in a straight
jacket at bedtime, so they
wouldn't have to monitor her
nightly meandering. We got her,
brought her, here to our home.
Nana is happy, she is unfettered
now, I am the one in the bind.

It Isn't Easy

It isn't easy,
this urge for change.
Takes moving
body and spirit.
I must escape, leave
all my duties, the
constant boredom,
abandon what's here.
Slip quietly away
to far-away spaces.
Places not seen before.
Wishful thinking, but
it isn't easy.

Colors My Day

Grayness through blue blinds
gray from morning until now
this bleak, desolate afternoon.
Quilt cover colors warm me
help me change gray day to
soft shades, multi colored.
It is tattered, frayed,
ragged, old like me.

Made of varied fabrics,
textures, silk and cotton
squares, hand stitched
together, made to huddle
under, cuddle for comfort.

I am still, yet my mind is
racing. Gray day outside
me here amid soft, warm
colors and a changing
cold, bleak, gray day.

Gwendolyn Brooks
at FCCJ February 7, 1987

Faces and bodies were
draped horseshoe around
her, they framed her.
Dark skinned woman
poet, she was 70 then.
She captivated the ones
with black hair coiled,
solemn straight, standing
blacks in suits, the white
faced, smooth haired, and
jean clad teens of all shades,
all here to see and hear her.

Her poems, words strung
together to be recalled.
Her lines stick and pop
out at colorless times.
Amazing, she was here
a 1950 Pulitzer Prize
winner. Her voice pure,
her simple words potent.

Her messages affecting
us all, drawing students,
teachers, visitors together.
She moved each one here.

Stretching us, word
strands connecting
readers, learners,
thinkers, all lovers of
words, all lovers of
this strong poet, with
such powerful words,
Gwendolyn Brooks.

Suburban Suite

A second of silence
all still outside, then
leaf blower whooshes,
siren wails cut the air,
lawn mower whirs
chain saw buzzing,
crows shrill cawing,
plane thundering, amid
steady slow drip drips
off eaves, plop drops
kids in street walking
high voices, young laughs
fade into a second of silence.

Wildlife Officer Kills Snakes at I-75 Rest Area
(Times Union, Sunday, May 24, 1987)

Reptiles misunderstood again,
symbols of evil since antiquity.
Forty-seven victims of Lee Crew's
maniacal revenge. Removed them
quick. "Forty-one were poisonous,"
they rationalized. Yes, and truckers,
tourists, travelers were nervous
sharing this natural woodland
with its rightful inhabitants.
Machete martyrs, these snakes were,
merely there to rest in their habitat.
It's now a blood-filled battlefield
where Crews, single-handedly
slew 47 loathed snakes as they
rested in I-75's rest area, one
specially not for them. Sacrifices
they were, though not many will
mourn, except snake lovers and me.
We'll grieve for all those reptiles
slayed at a rest area off Florida I-75.

Poetry Forms

The Rondelet

The Rondelet is a brief French form of poetry. It consists of one stanza, made up of seven lines. It contains a refrain, a strict rhyme scheme and a distinct meter pattern.

The word is from the diminutive of rondel, meaning round. This is the basic structure:

Line 1 A—four syllables
Line 2 b—eight syllables
Line 3 A—repeat of line one
Line 4 a—eight syllables
Line 5 b—eight syllables
Line 6 b—eight syllables
Line 7 A—repeat of line one

The refrained lines should contain the same words, however—substitution or different use of punctuation on the lines has been common.

All Shapes and Size

All shapes and size
classical forms I write and teach
all shapes and size
a form for all I fantasize
you need meter and rhyme, I preach
so many forms to use, try each
all shapes and size.

Richie Levine

Richie Levine
does research and writes every day
Richie Levine
creative screenwriter he's fine
his work is good, people do say
they'll come to watch and even pay
Richie Levine

The Cinquain

Created and developed by the American poet Adelaide Crapsey in the early 1900. It is a five-line unrhymed poem with 22 syllables arranged as 2, 4, 6, 8, and 2. Its name is derived from the French word *cinq* which means five.

The Cinquain is usually centered and has the following format:

First line: a noun, one-word subject or title, two syllables.

Second line: two adjectives which describe the subject, 4 syllables.

Third line: three verbs relating to the subject, six syllables.

Fourth line: four words, a phrase, sentence, or feelings relating to the subject, eight syllables.

Fifth line: one word which summarizes the poem or restates the subject, two syllables.

Feline
feral, hungry
exists, adapts, survives
waits patient for our cats' leftovers
porch cat

Writer
novice, learner
complains, explains, accepts
willing to work, rewrite, revise
author

Woman
unique, brainy
informs, details, suggests
methods, tactics, systems, success
winner

Maureen
honest, clever
appears, commits, advises
always ready to help others
doer

The Tanka

The tanka poem originated in the seventh century, one of the oldest forms of Japanese poetry. Tankas are short enough to allow for quick composition but long enough to allow for adequate emotional expression. Tanka poem is similar to Haiku but Tanka poems have more syllables and use simile, metaphor and personification. Tanka poems are written about nature, seasons, love, sadness and other strong emotions.

There are five lines in a Tanka poem.

Line one—5 syllables
Line two—7 syllables
Line three—5 syllables
Line four—7 syllables
Line five—7 syllables

white lightning flashes
now rain comes down fast gray sheets
loud thunder resounds
back cringing in war torn lands
seeing blood red death all 'round

for Jim

Pain smacks, sweat pours fast
heart attack can kill you now
speed to hospital
surgeon's skill technology
pain ceases you live today

Dreary day, feel lost
wander roads take random turns
sun slices light gray sky
diamond sparkles, calm ocean
vast water soothes weary soul

Winter sunny day
trees once flamed autumn hues
bare now, naked limbs
reaching out to deep blue sky
I stop to savor the scene

The Triolet

The triolet is a medieval French poetry form that has eight lines and was introduced to the English language by poets in the 17th century. The triolet is isosyllabic, all lines have the same number of syllables. The rhyme scheme is, ABaAabAB.

1. A
2. B
3. a Rhymes with 1st line.
4. A identical to 1st line.
5. a Rhymes with 1st line.
6. b Rhymes with 2nd line.
7. A Identical to 1st line.
8. B Identical to 2nd line.

Note that the lst, 4th, and 7th lines are identical. The 2nd and 8th lines are identical. Lines 3, 5, 6 are single, different.

Some Days Some Nights

Some days feel like night.
Some nights should be days
gray skies blur my sight.
Some days feel like night.
Nothing clear nor bright
yearning for sun rays.
Some days feel like night.
Some nights should be days.

Smiles

Smiles can make gray days brightly shine,
may even take away the blues.
Happier days may soon be mine,
smiles can make gray days brightly shine.
Now sadness gone all will be fine.
Look around and see all the clues.
Smiles can make gray days brightly shine
may even take away the blues.

My Dentures

My dentures do not fit quite right
they always come out when I eat.
Oh, what a horrifying sight
my dentures do not fit quite right.
It often happens at first bite
no matter if pasta or meat.
My dentures do not fit quite right
they always come out when I eat.

The Haiku

While some forms of poetry have free rein with regard to their subject or number of lines and syllables, the haiku was established in Japan as far back as the 9th century with a specific structure, style, and philosophy. Many poets still write in the original 5-7-5 syllable pattern and follow the traditional rules for writing haiku. Haiku poetry traditionally discusses abstract subjects or those from the natural world, including seasons, months and animals.

The structure of a traditional haiku is always the same, including the following features:

1. There are only three lines, totaling 17 syllables.
2. The first line is 5 syllables.
3. The second line is 7 syllables.
4. The third line is 5 syllables like the first.
5. Punctuation and capitalization are up to the poet, and need not follow the rigid rules used in structuring sentences.
6. A haiku does not have to rhyme, in fact usually it does not rhyme at all.
7. It can include the repetition of words or sounds.

brown dust, wet green grass
rising, whirling from the ground
mighty mower hurls

eye holder starers
microscopic onlookers
yet seeing nothing

hands behind his back
he walks steadfast in cold rain
harsh wind unheeded

loud screech of a tire
not a sweet trilling bird song
just man's rubber wail

gray moss moving slow
white shirt tail flap snap snapping
cycle wheels turning

high brown grass wavers
quick red ant climbs dying leaf
coldness is coming

The Clerihew

The clerihew, invented by Edmund Clerihew Bentley, consists of four lines rhymed aabb. The lines aren't of any particular length, and present a short biography.

It is a very specific kind of humorous verse. The first line contains a person's name. The verse is usually whimsical, showing the subject from an unusual point of view. It has four lines of irregular length. The rhyme structure is AABB. The meter and rhyme are often strained for humorous effect.

1. Pick a Subject—Clerihews are usually about a person, but not always and not necessarily a real person. The first line contains the person's name or the subject of the verse.

2. Make it AABB—There's only one hard and fast rule: AABB couplets. The first two lines rhyme and the second two lines rhyme.

3. Make a Point The second line sets up the premise and says something about the subject. Make it rhyme with the first line. It doesn't have to be true, or even make sense.

4. Add Context—The third and fourth lines add context to your premise, like the punchline to a joke. They should rhyme, but do not have to rhyme with the first two lines.

5. Make it Funny—The best clerihews are clever and sometimes sarcastic. They're not typically insulting or mean-spirited.

6. Make it Unpredictable—The uneven meter makes the form easy to write and adds to the whimsical charm. Lines may be of any length, from a single word to ten or more.

7. Don't Overthink It—Paul Ingram, owner of Prairie Lights Books in Iowa City and modern-day clerihew master, says "If it takes more than two minutes to think up, it isn't going to work."

Author and poet Paula R. Hilton
is not striving to be another Poe or Milton
yet she rewrites and revises each poem
omits words until she gets the right tone.

Artist and writer Jim Draper
went on a day long nature caper.
He saw a myriad of flowers and fauna
found this better than practicing Dhyāna.

Mystery writer Anne Perry
as a teen committed a felony
with her friend Pauline Parker,
they murdered Parker's mother with ardor.

Canadian writer Alan Bradley
his main character girl scientist Flavia sadly
stays eleven through his eleven-book series
of this he often ignores readers' queries.

The Pantoum

Introduced to Western poets by Victor Hugo, the Pantoum is a repeating fixed form from Malaysia. It is written in quatrains, in which the second and fourth lines of one quatrain become the first and third lines of the succeeding quatrain. There is no fixed line length or topic. Don't let all the lines confuse you. This is fairly simple if you follow the directions.

Step 1: Write the first four lines with or without a rhyme scheme of abab.
Step 2: Copy lines 2 and 4 to lines 5 and 7.
Step 3: Write lines 6 and 8 (rhyme = c).
Step 4: Copy lines 6 and 8 to lines 9 and 11.
Step 5: Write lines 10 and 12 (rhyme = d).
Step 6: Copy lines 10 and 12 to lines 13 and 15.
Step 7: Copy lines 3 and 1 to lines 14 and 16 (in that order).

Poets Pantoum

Poets see what others miss
they write their thoughts to share
wet leaf glistens with sun's kiss,
oh, look closely if you dare.

They write their thoughts to share
each word carefully selected
oh, look closely if you dare
words can make us sad or elated.

Each word carefully selected
crafting images dreary or bright
words can make us sad or elated
they want to show it right.

Crafting images dreary or bright
wet leaf glistens with sun's kiss
they want to show it right.
Poets see what others miss.

Flamingos, Dragons and Dragonflies

Flamingos,
dragons
and dragonflies
surround me in my study.
They hang, stand and sit
on my bookcases, dangle in
my three windows, one is
even nailed over my study door.

Flamingos, long sinewy necks,
sit and stand tall on bookcases,
sway in window, always
urge me to get in touch with
my emotions, my feelings.
They maintain harmony and
coherence between time,
space, and dimensions.
Flamingos calm, restore me.

Dragons with thick neck
spiked mains, grace shelves.
On top of black bookshelf
a large jade one. Under him
a gold gilded blue ceramic,
tail high, mouth wide creature.
Over my door an intricate
wooden circle dragon protects.
A quarter sized black pin dragon
leans against an amethyst rock.
Dragons most ancient, imposing,
bring out my fighting spirit.

Dragonflies, iridescent wings
swing from lamps, thick glass imprint
hovers over candle holder, magnifies
when lit. A tiny dragonfly barrette
on my amethyst plate. Dragonflies
soar 45 mph. Its message to me,
be energetic, open to life.
They symbolize light and
change, prompt me to open
my heart and mind to change.

All of them, flamingos, dragons
and dragonflies here in my study
remind me each day to love life,
my work, be productive, feel
relaxed even when life is difficult.

PC ah PC with a Maule
January 22, 1995

She sat and waited for death
not hers but part of her, her
mother's death slowly coming.
She forgot adventures in life,
forgot wafting over beaches,
touching down to go, to
go to freedom's heights.

It is the way it is up here
where everything is small,
vague, insignificant except for
sky, wind, water and how
black-green trees look from here.

She can see a spark, the start of
life's adventure in the gentle twists
at the hands of the strong sea captain
aloft. She is fearful of everything
this close to death, for so long.
Daily it separates strength, risks
and orgasms for they are life blood.

Flying here next to Pete, gently,
tenderly using the Maule's strength.
He is showing her to live in the hands
of a stranger, in an even stranger
pert carrier. She must be like the
Maule, pulling up strong, fast
hauling up, steady like a cantering
beast, the wild, short scraggily ones
on Cumberland type. She like the
Maule, rising like sea oats, shoot
up but strongly anchor the island.

This man steadily is leading her
into life's good times on her
half century birthday,
high in this cold winter sky.
He is showing to her innards,
shouting to her, over engine
sounds, telling her,
how clear, up here, life is.

It is the Maule on her best
days full of herself, like her,
in the blue sky over North
Florida pines, with him seeing the
sea, the woods and in small bits
seeing her, all in time to live again.

May 1996

May, already
it is hot,
muggy
can't move
kind of hot.
Sitting still
not budging
even to breathe
slumped, folded
into the river.
I can stop and let the
Altamaha run for me.

Seeking Solace

When feeling sad, lost and alone
I use this mood to create a poem.

Don't need to travel very far
can't now, don't drive a car.

Outside to my backyard I go
to hear nature's sounds, I know,

dove cooing, owl who-whoing
trees swaying, leaves rustling.

Here is where I always find
solace for my body and mind.

His Leaving
Joseph Allen Harlin, 25,
died January 17, 1999

My rebellious stepson spent his last
day doing the things, he enjoyed most.
He was with his friend Jeff and his
other Savannah buddies. He partied
at the beach drinking and drugging
from noon to midnight and then
Jeff poured him into the car.
Jeff and Jody were in the front
seat, Joe sprawled in the back.

"He left the car," as Jim genteelly
puts the exiting of his second son.
No one said they saw him leave.
Why he chose that moment will
always be a mystery, if he knew he
was leaving a moving car or if he
just in his stupor had to take a leak,
bullishly grabbed for the handle,
suddenly dropped to his death.

"He left the car," and his leaving has
left all of us numb. Anger, just pure
raging anger is what Jim is holding
back. His fog, his seeming serenity,
muffling his shrieks, silent screams,
for his troubled son, finally stilled.

No more middle of the night calls from the jail.
No more runs to the all-night laundromat to get
his boy out of the cold winter Jacksonville night.
No slit eyes insolently snagging a cigarette or a pack
or better yet a carton from Jim. No Joe to cart to the
treatment program, halfway house, Salvation Army.
Joe is gone. His hostility harnessed, encased in the
just bought coffin, planted near the Savannah River.

Death Drive to Dallas and Back
September 1999

Moaning, wailing, pleading
"No one will help me,"
saying this, she wore me
down. Her brother died,
she had to go, didn't drive.
Inner voices demanded
I do, demanded action.
So, I gladly responded,
heeded her incessant voice.
She wore me down repeating
all the things she was needing.
Depleting all my energy.
My departing spirit leaving
me with whispering voices.
Warning relentless voices.
While all the while her
voice was screaming
"Me. Me. Me."

Lovely Ladies

Elizabeth

She found her place
her own place, to share
with her dogs, her cats.
She found her voice, a
strong, keen, true voice.

She leads with high laugh,
deep red lipstick,
tattooed skin, arrayed in
flowing black clothes.
Alert mind, open intently
listening, befriending
crones, older women
with much to share.

Her cares, her time, myriad
hours spent on her work.
Her creations bring her joy,
satisfaction. Urge her to hard
work on a film with a purpose.

She teaches adults finding
their voice. She cleans for
other people. Her place too.
She is happy, joyous, free of
others draining debris. Left now
to make her life her own creation.

Elizabeth on her way making
unique films in her own name.

Allison

Something about stillness makes a girl sing
with warbling, lilting, proud on key voice,
"You can get it if you really want it."

She sings loudly, gesticulating, thrusting
her full five-year-old body toward her
audience. She sings forcefully to the
Hayward hills, cluttered with houses
filled with people. Her voice carries
to the Castro Valley grasses alive with
her music. A brown grass audience
swaying to her voice. She is a
melding of mammoth dark man,
who makes music and a finely
filigreed curly haired white woman.

Allison, proudly sings for me,
"You can get it if you really want it."
Fine like aged wine, girl child, woman
voice, over and over yet in the repetition
her voice stays firm. She repeatedly
hits notes precisely right each time,
"You can get it if you really want it."

Oh, what a mantra. What a litany.
She sings the truth for women not
yet taught to fear their strength,
their anger. They are our daughters'
determined voices, they sing for us.
She sings for us who hide our usness.

Lovely Ladies

Allison lays in the sun on the deck
with Sunny stretched long on her
side, next to Allison's backside.
Her curly black mass tinged with red
head spills on the retriever's golden
paws, her legs twitch. They both, now
warmed by the sun, stretch fully,
both switch and move their legs, like
Follies dancers. Both change positions,
paws first, then tiny, pudgy hands.

She lifts her head, shakes curls.
Dog moves, jumps up, unfurls.
The moment is broken, like the silence
when wind ripples through the chimes.

Marilyn's girl child, music and motion
warmth and cooling, soothing sounds
coming from girl child, woman voice.
Sing on sweet Allison, sing loudly,
"You can get it if you really want it."

Beth

In the 70s I saw a smiling wide
soft brown eyed lady, spring
into the room, noted the tuft of
black hair projected under her
lacy blouse arm, ah yes, she
was Casey, the grin lady.

Wherever she went
little trails of her were left
behind, a book, poem, a small
doo-dah found in a second
hand store, presents from her,
left in the wake of her whirling.

Plants, kittens and kids all came
to Ms. Fix-it KC, she can do it, give
it to her, fix a runny nose, pet
a purring cat, slip into a pretty hat.

Beth in a pair of khaki colored
shorts, brown legged booted KC
plowing gardens for old ladies,
red necked crackers, telling tall
tales, getting dirty, making things
grow as she gleefully goes.

Lovely Ladies

She lit up the dark walled
Riverside apartment, stood
in front of the oak mirror,
spread her thin arms out,
twirled about, in lace and satin
from Flea Market stalls, lady in
finery, at ease in work clothes, too.

Wise and woeful rattling on about
men, love and being herself. She
rode a motorcycle called Annabelle,
drove a dented VW called Seagull.
She sashayed through the restless
waiting game by never sitting still.

For decades she was my friend
until she married a Republican.
I haven't seen her since then.

Lisa

In her crisp black uniform,
shiny black shoes, gun belt
at her side, she is formidable.
Lisa can tell you code numbers,
knows correct procedure,
can write precise reports,
is compassionate and firm,
in the same instant. She can and
does think quickly on her feet,
sizes up situations with
lightning speed and accuracy.

She has no tolerance for
dishonesty, laziness, or
taking the easy way out.
She endures harassment
from her superiors in
small and monstrous ways.
It is not a pretty picture.

She is denied promotions
when she is more qualified
than the male who gets the higher
rank. No matter how competent
women are, the "good old boys"
always pull strings and win.

Lovely Ladies

Shared sad eyed stories of the
black bearded man, we both
knew. We read together in a
one bedroom apartment, on
the ocean, overflowing with
sunshine on a white bedspread
covered, brass and iron bed.

You made vegetable feasts,
I ate heartily all you cooked.
You are a red faced lovely
bearing blueberry muffins.
Early morning lady, fluid
like the sea, you are my calm.
Dreaming of you in warm beach
skies, dissatisfaction driven away.
Drift my way again soon, please.

Trying

Trying to stop worrying.
Trying to write about now.
Trying to not let all this
effort trying, get me down.
Trying to just sit here and
write the things in my head.

at 75 All the Same
January 20, 2020

She shimmers in when needed
three quarters of a century old.
Makes a wish for rain to match
her mood, on this gray cool,
damp dismal, January afternoon.

Her brain sizzles pops and
cracks as she turns each
lettered page waiting for her
pencil to scratch out words,
move sentences around
look for the inner core.
Can the story be found?

This year's start was death
defying. His heart clogged.
Stent inserted he lives.

Lesser drama but still
disturbing disaster.
Rhiannon's pipes burst
water spurts and plumber
came. It is all the same,
no big difference, even
though she's three
quarters of a century old.

No More Good Moves

Each time I lose at
Solitaire, a sign says,
"No more good moves."
Would we heed this
if it happened in life?
A stop sign.
A fire wall.
Avoid this pitfall.
"No more good moves."

Do I know what to do?
Do I? Now, what's next?
A rest, go back, choose
to turn in direction?

Knowing I have no
more good moves
isn't enough
information.
It leads to more
questions, more
dilemmas, more
problems in life.

Not so in Solitaire,
I just start a new game.

Hubird and Liz

Mornings bring chirps through
sun streaks. Hubird, canary,
sits mute, while Liz, his
loquacious mate, trills.
Female canaries are not
supposed to sing. Laying
eggs her forte' until separate
cages gave her a melodious
voice. All the library books
state, "Males are the singers,
females lay eggs" and chirp.
Liz is a hermaphrodite,
singing loudly, proudly laying
eggs. Prolific layer without nest.
Her feathers, dirty, muted yellow.
Hubird's, shiny, crisp dark yellow,
frothier feathers, puffy silk like.
She nervously skitters and hops.
He puffs out fully, perches calm.
Before she came, he sang robust,
never stopped, puffing, trilling
reaching heights of symphonic
bursts. Then when she came
he pouted, stopped singing, sat
silent on his perch, sickly white.
She chirped madly and littered
her cage. Eggs here, eggs there.
He got an abscess and died.
Liz kept laying eggs and singing.

Summer Daze

Sun is shining,
breeze is blowing.
Sky is darkening
trees are swaying.
I sit here waiting
for the rain.

Murder Mouse

White, pink, soft, fluffy
you run round your wheel
first forward slowly, then
slide backward, missing a
beat, cre-ak, creak, sque-ak.

Your cage is small,
floor covered with food,
green and seedy. You had,
a mate but you ate her. We
watched you gobble her up.

Cre-ak, creak, sque-ak, squeak
round you run. Off the wheel
you eat, drink, defecate,
then back on the wheel,
cre-ak, creak, sque-ak, squeak.

Sunday, it rained, no sounds
from the wheel, we looked in,
saw you still, huddled, sickly
at the bottom of littered cage.
Your body was bloated,
coat no longer fluffy.

You didn't use the wheel.
No one ate you, Murder
Mouse, you just died.
No more cre-ak, creak, sque-ak.

Skeleton Remnants

See the skeleton remnants
pieced together, tenses
melding what is it,
was it, what will it be?
Does willing make it so?

Flashes brought by muted
wings, a coral-colored beak.
What was this? she says it
laughing, to catch the cry.
The howl holed up in her
throat. It's better not to care
about what your cares are.

Rushes, minute etchings,
painfully dredged,
forced to living color.
Discs carefully selected,
each turn significant.

Stars on Water

Sunlight strikes
stars on water
rainbows in puddles
on rain-soaked streets.

A blink a whir, flutter
dragonfly wings
swish by, shine deep
blue sparkle flying
swift flashes swirl
around all around.

All the world shines
when sun hits the rain.
World whirls with color
when bright sunshine
comes after dark rain.

My Gratitude List

Today I am grateful for
all my beloved family,
friends who are like family,
my life, my words, love.
Grateful for this dreary, hot,
humid September Florida day.
Grateful for this community
of writers, poets, artists and
all who appreciate things created
by mere mortals on this troubled earth.
I am thankful for the writers who trust
me with their words, who listen to
suggestions and who I see and
hear their stories grow and glisten.

Flickers Dance

We buy sunflower seeds to keep
wild birds in our yard. Today
my morning view outside the
kitchen window is the mating
dance of these woodpeckers.
Erotic movements, loud chattering,
wik, wik, wik, a whistle *peeah*,
sounds from the winged flickers.

Flashy male, red nape, black mustache,
black crescent on his breast, underparts
tan, with lots of black spots. She
is smaller, with muted colors, both
have same barred gray-brown and
black back with a white rump.

They bob and stretch, tightrope
hop on the tree's lowest branches.
They stop, stand frozen, for
seconds, (I count to twenty)
their frenetic movement
begins again. They separate,
dance, then freeze again, move,
continue their courtship dance.

Mesmerized I stand still at the
kitchen sink. Don't want to
miss a moment, of this pairing.
Laundry, dishes, weekly chores
give way to this unexpected gift.

A Gentle Nag

Get out of your head
look under the bed.

Get out of your robe
slip into some clothes.

Don't hide inside
open the door wide.

Let sunlight warm you
your dogs need sun, too.

Stretch your arms out
twirl round, see all about.

You have it all now, girl
time to enjoy the whirl.

Yes, girl know it,
come on show it.

This world is yours.

Dead Weight

She sags, sighs
she sheds friends
instead of pounds
shucks them off
like oyster shells
verbally pulls them apart
so, they too, hastily depart.
Then she jerks with a start
disgruntled yet free
of irritating debris,
folks who said they cared
about the tales she shared
    but only sucked her dry
with all their woes and try
        as hard as she could
nothing she did ever would
be more important to them
              than them.

Rusty Spigot

I am a rusty spigot
only let my poems out
in trickles, irregular spurts.
No images, only a thicket
of banal words I spout.
Raucous sounds I blurt.

Cauldron of Thoughts

A cauldron of thoughts
roils, boils, bubbles.
No calm, none sorted out.
She simmers, wonders
what is going on? Or off?

Things happening, too
many changes in her life.
Inside, outside her whirl.
One thing remains same,
her terror of reality.

Others can just go through
each day getting buffeted,
bashed upon the rocks
of real life. Resilient,
they bounce right into
all of life's daily doings.

She gets morose, wants
to hide not go anywhere.
She didn't used to be
this bad but now she
doesn't see much good
in going through the
"civilities" in an
otherwise, uncivil world.

Eggs Boiling and Aging

The eggs shaking,
rattling in the pan
made me have to pee.
Yee gads I'm not sorry
how I've treated my body
but so sorry what a joke
this time of life is and
how aware I am of
mechanisms I wish
to be unaware of.

at 76 Hopeful
January 20, 2021

Unite if we dare.
It's a grand day
for me and our country.
It is time to reach out,
mend our decaying land,
calm our troubled woes.

At 76 I am hopeful,
aware of all the rot
needing to be repaired.
All the damage the ruthless
leader left behind, all the
disenfranchised needing help,
all the rebels left with despair.

Out with the liar, bigot, whiner,
crafty crook, tantrum maker,
destroyer of democracy.
In with a positive message
for every American who
wants true unity and peace.

A new beginning to end
the pandemic plaguing
our people, to soothe the
sick and hopeless, to
remember the dead and
all those they left behind.

Name Changes

Born in 1945
Lynn Marie Langevin
adopted by Skapyak
married Glenn, divorced
Skapyak again
married Lee, divorced
Skapyak again
married Daley, divorced
Skapyak again
met, loved Harlin
married again, 1995
now 2022 still
Lynn Skapyak Harlin

Just Now

My mind floats
    like pollen
in the air.
Everything coated
    in yellow dust.
There are so many
    things I should
do but my mind
       is floating.

Old Friends Gone

Some dead
     some lost
some just not
    here anymore.
They are alive
    in my study,
with me now.
     Peering down
from their frames
    with smiles,
full laughs.
They are vivid
    in my mind.
Their voices
    caress my ears.
Their steps resound
footfalls, distinctive.
Old friends,
    bodies gone, yet
spirits never,
     ever forgotten.

at 77 Seeking Joy
January 20, 2022

I look for joy.
I have heat, A/C, a strong roof
overhead, food in the running
refrigerator, water, all I really need.

This year I start with hope, optimism,
anticipation, courage, faith and confidence.
I swat away despair, misery, desolation,
anguish, gloom, dejection, and the
bleakness, and harshness all round me.

This year my words are joy and gratitude.
I am grateful for all the people in my life.
I find happiness with each of them.
I am thankful for my family, friends,
the writers I work with, all who bring
me joy. I am happy to be alive at 77.

About the Author

Lynn Skapyak Harlin, poet, writer, and editor worked as an educator for 20 years. She taught English, Journalism, AP and Standard classes 7-12 in Duval County. As an instructor at Florida State College Jacksonville and Jacksonville University, Lynn taught Language Arts, Writing Seminars and Adult Education. She conducted adult education classes in Nassau and Duval Counties, as well as creating and conducting training programs for corporate and government employees.

Between teaching jobs, to keep her sanity, she sailed in the Netherlands as a mate on a traditional Dutch tjalk (pronounced chalick), a steel sailing ship, and saw North America as a cross country truck driver for North American Electronic & Exhibitions Division.

She led a Poetry Workshop with Sharon Scholl and Carolee Bertisch for four years at the Florida Heritage Book Festival. She presented her work at First Coast Writers Conference and at the National Institute of Critical Thinkers in Boston, San Francisco and Chicago. Her programs and poetry have been presented all over the country.

As a reporter and photojournalist for publications in South Georgia and North Florida she tackled subjects as diverse as restaurant reviews, community features and crime news. A freelance writer for thirty years, her writing has been published in textbooks, trade magazines, literary magazines, newspaper articles and features.

Her first published poem, "War Waste", appeared in *Time*, (December 7, 1970). Her poems have appeared in *The Aquarian, Gate, State Street Review, Shakespeare's Cat Café, Arbus, Women's Voices, Section Eight Magazine, Florida Speaks, AC PAPA vol.1, 2 & 3* (Ancient City Poets, Authors, Photographers and Artists), deadpaper.org and ashandbones.com.

Two chapbooks of Lynn's poetry, *Real Women Drive Trucks* (1997) and *Press One for More Options* (1997), were published by Closet Books. Her chapbook, *Age Changes* (2017), was published by Happy Tapir Press. Her collection of 90 poems, *Twists and Turns* (2019) was published by Hidden Owl, LLC.

For 16 years she held writers workshops on her shantyboat docked at Seafarers Marina on the Trout River. In 2017 Hurricane Irma destroyed her beloved refuge and left only the back deck and the gangway.

Lynn lives in Jacksonville, Florida with her husband, Jim Harlin, and her standard poodle, Beau Brummel, where she continues to write and rewrite her poems. She now conducts writers' workshops on Zoom and hopes to be able to hold them in her home again soon. She measures her success by the progress of her writers.

You may contact her at lyharlin@aol.com

Books Edited by Lynn Skapyak Harlin

Lynn became Senior Editor of Closet Books in 2001 and edited Jacksonville University Professor Emeritus Sharon Scholl's two poetry collections, *Unauthorized Biographies* (2002) and *All Points Bulletin* (2004). During this time, she also edited *Women's Voices* and *Men's Voices* (2001), Robert Gantt *The Crows* (2001), Tonn Pastore *Convergence* (2003) and many other poets' work.

Starting in June 2003, Lynn worked with former, First Coast News anchor Donna Deegan (then Hicken) while she wrote her first book *The Good Fight* (2004) and *Through Rose Colored Glasses* (2009) which Lynn edited and were published by Closet Books. All the proceeds benefit the Donna Foundation which helps First Coast women and men living with breast cancer.

Lynn has edited numerous award-winning authors' work, among which include Erwin Wunderlich, first place winner of Florida Historical Society's best historical fiction award (2009), Rick Maloy, whose short stories won (2007) and placed (2008) in the Florida First Coast Writers' short fiction contests and noted artist and writer, Oscar Senn, whose novel placed third (2003) and short story won (2002) and placed (2006) in the Florida First Coast Writers' short fiction contests.

She edited the poetry collection of Carolee Ackerson Bertisch *Who Waves the Baton?* (2005), North Florida Writers *Word Trips, Poems from the First Coast* (2007), Tonn Pastore *Mark My Words* (2018), Ben Atkinson *Spider Lightning* (2019), John Rowland *One Foot in Front of the Other* (2019), Robert Gantt *Songs from the Cage* (2019) and Paula R. Hilton *At Any Given Second* (2020).

Lynn also edited several memoirs, fiction and nonfiction books during the past 20 years. She has coached and edited many local writers' manuscripts. Most notable, portrait artist Ann Manry Kenyon's coffee table book, *Memories, Method & Mastery: A Memoir of a Life in Art* (2016) which chronicles her life, with 100 of her paintings done over the years. Media personality Tracy Collins *Stumbling into Sobriety* (2018), Atlanta resident, retired surgeon, Jeff Jones *Our Universe: A Journey into Mystery* (2018), Erwin Wunderlich *Drummer Boy on the Run* (2019), Mike C. *Daily Flight Plan* (2019) and *Daily Departure Plan* (2021), Carlos M. Cruz *Watching a Policy Maker's Back as Well as Your Own* (2019), Sarah W. Crooks *Home Is Here, Along Red Pearl River* (2020), retired GSU Professor, Susan Easterbrooks, *My Time with Ela Gandhi* (2020) and Craig R. Seaton *Some Perfect Tomorrow* (2021).

She loves the challenge of helping writers see their words in print.

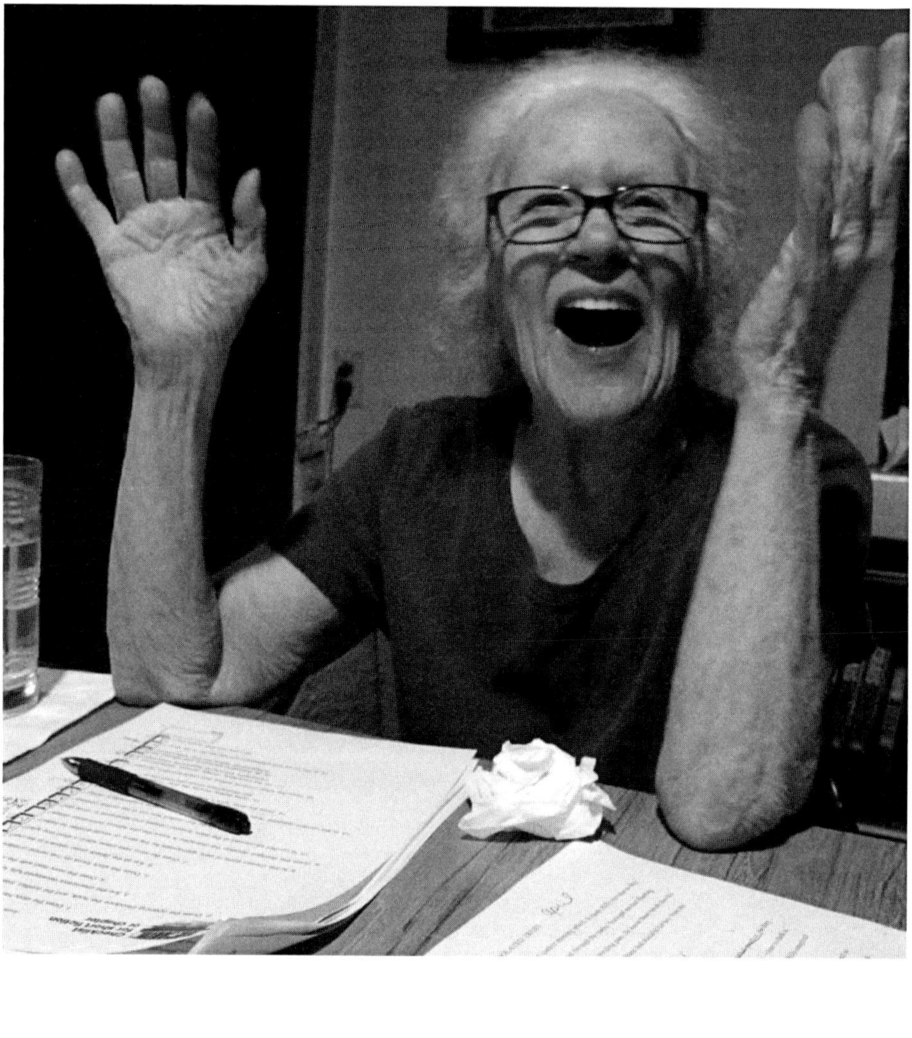